Following The Tide

By Tiayana Edgar

Library For All Ltd.

Following The Tide

First published 2022

Published by Library For All Ltd
Email: info@libraryforall.org
URL: libraryforall.org

Our Yarning logo design by Jason Lee, Bidjipidji Art

Original illustrations by Caitlyn McPherson

Following The Tide
Edgar, Tiayana
ISBN: 978-1-922849-57-1
SKU01354

Following the Tide

We respect and honour Aboriginal and Torres Strait Islander Elders past, present and future. We acknowledge the stories, traditions and living cultures of Aboriginal and Torres Strait Islander peoples on this land and commit to building a brighter future together.

"School's out!"

It was the last day of school. I called out to my cousins as we ran out of the gates to Mum's car.

"Let's go to the beach!"

When we arrived, the tide was on the way out.

"Look! Catch the tide!" Mum said. We started racing towards the water.

4

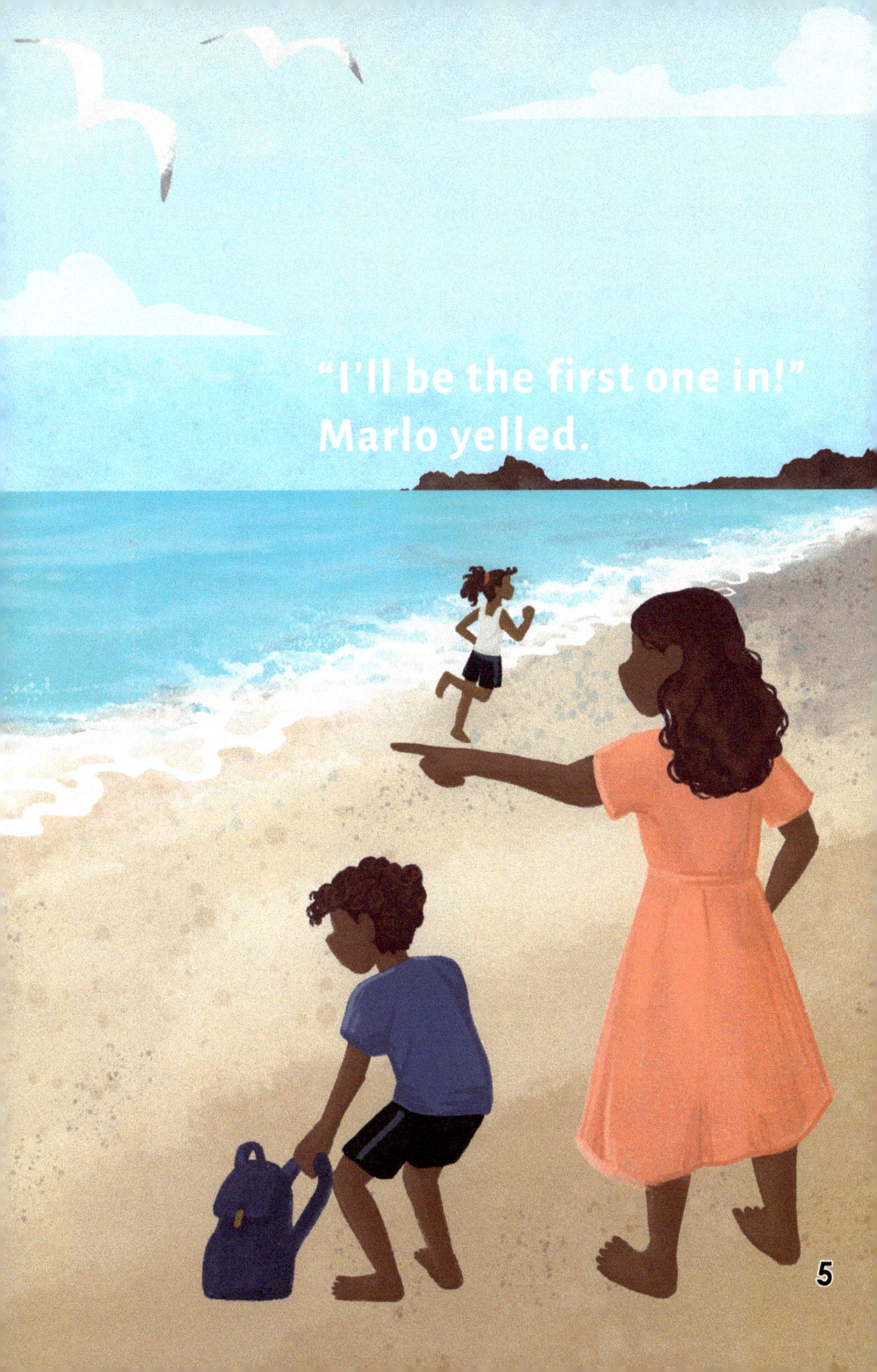

“I’ll be the first one in!” Marlo yelled.

The water was nice and cool.
I loved feeling the water rush
around my body as I dived in and
out of the waves. The mangroves
brushed against our legs.

But as we got deeper into the mangroves, the water got higher. "We need to find somewhere higher, too," Marlo said.

Then we saw a big piece of white foam that had drifted into the mangroves. We all jumped on and pushed it around, floating on top of the water.

When I looked down into the water I saw lemon sharks, stingrays, small fish and even mud crabs. They were all heading out, following the tide.

"Time to come in now," said Mum.
"That tide's going out fast!"

The tides near us can be dangerous.
If you're not paying attention, you
might get swept out to sea!

Suddenly, our foam board
bumped onto a sandbar.

"Phew," I said, smiling at my cousins. "We're safe. Let's go back and get some mayi." Our parents were happy to see us back on shore.

That afternoon we gathered bush food, oysters, shellfish, small fish, and mud crabs, to have a big feed.

Our parents helped us cook up
the food. We had a rest as the
sun went down.

Did you know....

Mayi is the word for 'food' in the Bardi language.

Tides in the Kimberley region of Western Australia are up to 11 metres and can be fast, dangerous and scary if you are in the water.

You can use these questions to talk about this book with your family, friends and teachers.

What did you learn from this book?

Describe this book in one word. Funny? Scary? Colourful? Interesting?

How did this book make you feel when you finished reading it?

What was your favourite part of this book?

About the author

Tiayana Edgar was born in Derby and now lives in Ardyaloon, north of Broome. She loves fishing and sharing stories with her family. The tides in Ardyaloon are huge and fast so it's important to watch carefully and move quickly.

Our Yarning

Want to discover more books from this collection? Our Yarning is a collection of books written by Aboriginal and Torres Strait Islander peoples across Australia.

We know that children learn better, and enjoy reading more, when they see themselves in the stories, characters and illustrations of the books they read.

To download the app, visit the Google Play Store on any Android device and search 'Our Yarning'.

www.ingramcontent.com/pod-product-compliance
Lightning Source LLC
Chambersburg PA
CBHW042344040426

42448CB00019B/3398

*9 7 8 1 9 2 2 8 4 9 5 7 1 *